HELPLESS ANGELS

HELPLESS ANGELS

TOM WAYMAN

for Angela —
with best wishes
from
Tom 5/17

thistledown press

Thistledown Press Ltd.
410 2nd Avenue North
Saskatoon, Saskatchewan, S7K 2C3
www.thistledownpress.com

Library and Archives Canada Cataloguing in Publication

Wayman, Tom, 1945-, author
Helpless angels / Tom Wayman.

Poems.
ISBN 978-1-77187-131-0 (softcover)
I. Title.

PS8595.A9H46 2017   C811'.54   C2017-901110-3

Cover and book design by Jackie Forrie
Printed and bound in Canada
Author photo by Jude Dillon

Canada Council   Conseil des Arts
for the Arts   du Canada

Canada

Thistledown Press gratefully acknowledges the financial assistance of the Canada Council for the Arts, the Saskatchewan Arts Board, and the Government of Canada for its publishing program.

For the musicians:

Thanks for the joy that you've given me
— *Mentor Williams*

CONTENTS

Mine was the first generation in history that became able to hear anyplace our choice of music performed by someone else. In the middle of the last century, while I was growing up, ordinary people often sang together as part of the fabric of everyday life. Every public meeting began with the audience singing "O Canada" and ended with the group intoning "God Save the Queen" (prior to 1953, "God Save the King"). In Boy Scouts, in mandatory choir at school, my voice was raised with others in song. I remember an assembly in junior high school in Prince Rupert, B.C. where all us boys were given detention because the principal didn't think we were singing "O Canada" with enough enthusiasm at the start of the event. During the national anthem, the principal complained, all he could hear were the alto and soprano voices of the girls.

An adult party in the 1950s usually included a sing-along. Magazine advertisements for a product promising quick mastery of piano-playing assured prospective buyers that a purchase would guarantee social success. Being adept at the piano would make you the life of the party because everyone would gather around you when the singing started. Bing Crosby's Academy Award-winning 1951 hit "In the Cool, Cool, Cool of the Evening," written by Hoagy Carmichael and Johnny Mercer, offers a glimpse into that culture of people making their own music:

> In the cool, cool, cool of the evening
> Tell 'em I'll be there
> In the cool, cool, cool of the evening
> Save your pappy a chair
> When the party's getting a glow on
> And singing fills the air
> In the shank of the night when the doings are right
> You can tell 'em I'll be there

and later

> If there's gas in my hack
> And my laundry is back
> If there's room for one more
> And you need me, why sure
> If you need a new face, or a tenor or bass . . .
> Well you can tell 'em we'll be there

The invention of the portable radio, however, meant that suddenly everywhere we carried the device we could listen to music that did not originate with our friends', neighbours', school classmates' or Scout troop's voices and/or musical instruments. A different relationship with music was born. As radios became smaller and smaller, they could more easily accompany us to any location. I recall lugging a leather-covered radio the size of a lunch-bucket to junior high school in order to listen at noon to the World Series, as well as popular songs. Later, small plastic radios would fit into a shirt pocket.

Even so, one limiting characteristic in those days of listening to music not made by ourselves was that away from our own or the family record player, or from a café jukebox, we were at the mercy of the choices of radio station DJs and record programmers regarding what reached our ears. To ease this transition, early radio stations encouraged listener input into the playlist, much like how the comments section following Internet news stories provide the illusion that consumers of news have some voice concerning what happens in the world. CFPR, CBC Radio's station in Prince Rupert, sponsored a weekly poll of the town's secondary students when I was in junior high to determine the current Top Twenty hit songs. Based on the poll results, a certain program each week aired a countdown, playing the songs in ascending order from number twenty to the most popular record. I remember that one week somebody in the high school organized a push-back and the town's young people managed to vote the McCulloch chain saw advertising jingle onto the local hit parade:

> With McCulloch you're the master
> 'Cause you keep on cutting faster:
> You're in luck when you got a McCulloch chain saw.

The station duly accepted the vote and played the tune when its ranking decreed, but not long after phased out the weekly survey.

My generation grew into adolescence constantly enjoying rock and roll, along with the musical cross-currents that influenced rock in its formative stages: folk, Tin Pan Alley, calypso, blues, gospel, country. Yet whenever you listened to the radio in your car or at the beach you had to wait for your favourite tune—or, when you were part of a romance, for "our song"—to be played. You could phone in requests to radio stations or particular programs. But mostly you didn't, enduring patiently the DJ's selections of bubblegum music and merely so-so recordings until at last you were rewarded by the opening chords of some song whose melody, lyrics, or both were currently significant for you.

Eventually, miniaturization of personal playback devices such as the in-car tape player and the Walkman allowed us to select our own music no matter where we were. Technology has continued to tweak that initial great shift that allowed us to surround ourselves everyplace outside the home with music performed by others. For me, thanks to this shift, music has been an important component of my life even though, after early training in piano, choral singing, clarinet and music theory, I play no instrument. And I sing only when nobody else is present, except for joining in on labour movement hymns on appropriate occasions.

Music by others, never far away, has functioned for my entire life as solace, inspiration, escape, memory-jogger. The music I love alters, creates and enhances my mood. The poems of the present volume, *Helpless Angels*, pay tribute to music's vital and omnipresent contribution to my enjoyment of life: generating in me a sense of happiness, excitement or well-being, or a gained or regained perspective on myself or on some encountered difficulty, or a continued encouragement to work toward a juster, fairer world for us all. Since English poetry on the page or in the ear began as song lyric, *Helpless Angels* intends as well to honour by implication its art form's origin, even though the appearance and content of most poems have changed a good deal from the era when poetry consisted of verses to be sung.

The poems gathered here intersect with music in a number of ways, mirroring the art form's range of interactions with my life. Some poems in *Helpless Angels* take music itself as their subject. Other poems, since one possible/impossible aim of contemporary poetry is not to write *about* a subject but to write the *subject*, intend to be song-like in feeling or content.

Some poems here explore the music of nature: how wind, water, earth and sky, often subjects for music, contain musical elements themselves. And music is nothing if not structured time: each piece announces, before it begins to flow along the stave, how the specific tune will organize and measure time. So time is the focus of many poems in *Helpless Angels*, including how a completed life reveals a structure perhaps not visible before life's end, how we experience and process irrevocable loss, and what it means to make music on a doomed planet in a universe that, at least according to some cosmologists, is no less destined for extinction.

Meanwhile music, as it passes through time both literally and figuratively, often provides us with the sense of a journey, of being transported to some other place. Mentor Williams' 1973 hit, "Drift Away," performed by Dobie Gray, embraces this metaphor of travel:

> And when my mind is free
> You know a melody can move me
> And when I'm feeling blue
> The guitar is coming through to soothe me

Thanks for the joy that you've given me
I want you to know I believe in your song
And rhythm and rhyme and harmony
You help me along, making me strong

Oh, give me the beat, boys, and free my soul
I want to get lost in your rock-and-roll
And drift away

So some poems here are road songs. Wrapped in a cocoon of engine, tire and wind-over-the-airframe sounds, with the dotted line of the road markings pulsing staccato or, in their reversion to a solid line, indicating a glissando, and with the vehicle cabin filled all the while with a favourite song flowing from the speakers, I have experienced decade after decade an emotional link between being behind the wheel on the open highway and the delights music can bring.

Wherever we are en route to, speeding across the earth and/ or through time, the pleasures music provides simultaneously are of the moment—accumulating note upon note—and reverberate long and far through our lives even once the specific sounds are silent. This is the wonder that the poems of *Helpless Angels* intend to depict, emulate and celebrate.

"Appledore"
Winlaw, B.C.
April 2015

INSTRUMENT

We haven't finished hearing
all the guitar has to say

to us
        Notes vibrato
        amid the rhythms of the
        chord changes
        —circular, oscillatory,
        picaresque
whether six string or twenty-six
string: the hard chairs
for the deputation waiting to speak
to city council, of the union hall,
community hall; people linking arms
as they stand on the court house steps, lawn
of the legislature; the dust and litter backstage
the audience never sees
        Minor chords of broken
        love, broken strikes, trumpet of
        resistance to legal war, the embraced violin
        of the unfolding rose
        Major chords
of rescue from coaltown flames, of the merciless executions
of the Communards, the oppressed's carnival
masks, peaty whisky
        —everything the support arm of the microphone stand
        leans in to hear:

air released in a burst or
scattered in shards

that take the shape of a hammer,
breast, a driving wheel, bacon and eggs,
    a house Jesus avoided,
      jackknifed semitrailer, cottonwood leaves,
      the twenty-seventh of November,
a woman stepping from a ferryboat onto shore

ONE TIME

Just once to hear
the tremulous yearning
in the words alone: *O pain,*
why can you not love me
as a mother, forgiving all?
while the syllables,
clauses, the systole, diastole
propel the living forward
into a country
where snow shines on distant ridges,
O pain, or the storm mists float aloft
on the valley walls, shrouding
the peaks, *O pain,* or clouds lower toward
the river, *why can you not love me*
as I love myself?

        And in that chain
of words alone, no music, a B-train or C-train
hauls overland through the fierce weather
O pain of spring, steering across the unloving, pitiless
injustice, and the energy, the desire
to defy it. How brave we are *O pain*
to travel these routes, the highway forward
why can we not love ourselves braiding,
rejoining, soaring through crossroads
as if we knew *star and chimney smoke*
what to love in one another, that country
—words
one time alone.

BLUE NORTH

Jesse Winchester (1944-2014)

1

Some of his songs are a vaulted hall
architected of sunlight
—others a canvas pavilion
open to rural air on every side.

It's true the black constructs of war, of
a conscripted soldiery, including a forced migration
of young people to freedom across an unfamiliar border
flow like a bass line

below the tones, the harmonies he crafted
as no singer eschews a minor key or chord.
But to enter his rhythms and lyrics was a respite
from our chanting of slogans in the tense avenues

of resistance, and the earlier hours arguing strategy
and tactics, laying out the poster, the pamphlet
until the words of the distant figure at the microphone
were erased by the motorcycles of the police.

His music, after the sit-in, the arrests
and the collection of bail money, was an afternoon
watching shore birds dart among the foam, or a hike
into the dry autumn hills, leaves crackling under our boots

before the evening rally at city hall. His stance
resembled the buttons always pinned to our shirts
freighting the conversation on any topic over spaghetti and beer
with the war, injustice, our determination

to help birth a fairer world.

2

Through our defeats
and small successes
he continued singing. This April his songs
float free of him.

Five mares graze the newly sprouted grass
in a field edged by leafing aspen
and birch. The high whistled buzz of a pine siskin
travels for a moment across the warming air.

Fingers strike strings, and a guitar begins
to unroll a message written long ago
but fashioned new each time. The notes
ascend and descend the staves, the clefs

like any of us behind the wheel
driving the hills and cutbanks of the two-lane
through the green season, the measured beats to the bar
flashing past like utility poles, fence lines edging the forest

and towns whose parking lots and lawns
retain a few mounds of melting snow.
His music, while we live
does not age, reveals despite its joy

how moral decisions are
common as bread, as salt, how all our days
our choices sing to us
of the land to which we go.

HEAVY WEATHER

Thunderclouds power into the valley
    Around the ridges to the south
Some here believe the darkness full of money
    Others, the pure light

    At the fair, the badmen ballads
        Roll again from the stage
    In front of the speakers, young women dance
        With their toddlers, mother and child swaying leg to
          leg

Thunderclouds loom over the valley
    —A contagion that advances from the south
Some believe this darkness is bearing money
    Others, the redeeming light

    Around the dancers, booths of canvas and wood
        Sell garlic and absolution
    The young husbands stand at the crowd's edge
        Speaking to each other of engines

Thunderclouds release the crumbling bass
    That precedes the downpour
Some believe the shadow full of benediction
    Others, unending night

    On the water, ripples swell into surf
        Fishers gun toward distant harbours
    On the mountain, beside the passing line of pickups and
        sedans
        Autumn's first snow dwindles on the shoulder

Thunderclouds push in from the south
    Some here are certain the darkness means wealth
Others, eternal chastisement from what brandishes rain and fire
    Still others, the abiding light

FRED NEIL AND THE RAINBOW

Summer's last day—the late Fred Neil's
12-string bass voice
resounds through the highway S-curves walled by fir, birch, pine
as, beyond the hayfield that is Lebahdo Flats,
a rainbow
touches the clump of cottonwood, vine maple, spruce
among which cluster the café and gas pumps
the shrunken river slides past.

The arch of gauzy color
pours down on the crossroad businesses' roofs
where Cedar Creek culverts under the asphalt
to join the larger stream: Fred Neil's booming scat
become droplets of fire a little bit of rain
is transposing into an arpeggio of light.

SONG

Wind came down the mountain
      Looking for something.
            He pushed at a swaying alpine fir, a pine

In case a branch or trunk could be ripped free to topple
      Onto snow. Further toward the valley bottom,
            He tousled the long stems of last year's meadow
            grasses

Sticking out from the drifted white
      Because he knew it irritated them, found a stand of leafless
      cottonwood
            With root rot, sick limbs

And left a tangle of blowdown. Where a highway sped through the
      valley
      He shook a semitrailer, then another
            As they rolled past snow heaped against slatted
            fences,

And managed to force a small station wagon
      Toward the road's shoulder for a moment
            Before the tires jerked back into true.

Fun, he thought. Then he saw a hawk
      Leave from a spruce aloft on a snowy ridge.
            I love to be with hawks,

He said, soaring up to coast next to the bird.
      I'm really an honorary hawk. I don't like eagles:
            They're arrogant, but have no reason

To imagine themselves superior. They're garbage hounds
  Same as their second cousins, the crows and ravens,
    Whom I also dislike: complainers, opportunists,

Low class. I know a hawk will stoop
  To eat a mouse, but nothing with blood is pure
    As me, and hawks at least acknowledge what they
    lack,

Aren't proud of it, feel honored when I glide beside them
  While they bank and lift: perfect as anything
    That isn't wind.

RICHIE HAVENS (1941-2013)

1

A noisy art-opening party in a house in Syracuse:
my friends the writer Dennis Saleh and his wife Michele
find him alone in the kitchen, leaning against
the sink. He never mentions, as they chat,
how he came to be there. But Dennis notices
a small gourd suspended among the beaded necklaces
the singer wears. *Soil from Bethlehem*, he explains,
and Dennis asks if he can touch it, and Havens
smiles and says, *Go ahead.*

2

An urgency in how his lyrics sound
all his life, but he began when we did
in a confused time, a time of resistance
     Hey, look yonder, tell me what you see
hunched over my turntable
to first listen to his voice
     Marching to the fields of Vietnam
as the sea wind flows through the rooms
in the California beach town where I lived
my days filled with the aromatic beauty of
     Looks like Handsome Johnny with a M15
bougainvillea, and with committee meetings, protest meetings
pickets, leaflets, posters, marches
     Hey, it's a long hard road, it's a long hard road
     It's a long hard road, hey, before we'll be free
—the cities burning far away, and up at Watts again
Che gunned down, and Fred Hampton
     Looks like Handsome Johnny with his hand rolled in a fist

And what we did was never enough
Bullets ending the argument at Kent State, Jackson State
  Marching to the Birmingham war, hey, marching to the
    Birmingham war

Even his tender lines vibrated
with how intensely we were buoyed
on the surf of flesh
  Sandy made me promise
  Not to tell
  Not a soul must know
  How well we loved

3

Something of the Old Testament
in his conviction: Jackson Browne's
blood on the wire brought forward
to Iraq, or the cry of Dino Valenti
from Quicksilver Messenger Service
who when he thought of his generation,
the choices we rejected, sensed the future trembling
—that shaking which the prophets knew
can never be entirely suppressed, and at its peak
moves the heavens and the ocean and the land.
Yet Havens' voice also conveyed
the weary understanding of Scripture's authors
that our failings, the losses and defeats,
are natural to a human life: he made a psalm of
Bob Lind's depiction of the man kissing his beloved
forever, while she kisses him goodbye.
And a plaintive psalm of a Kris Kristofferson composition
—how we try and stumble at love, social justice
or any desired good

yet in the end have to accept that for some of us
the venture is what our life was:

> *Storm on the mountain,*
> *Stars in the sky.*
> *Running for glory,*
> *Freedom to fly.*

The hymns Havens crafted
are borne aloft on many voices, but now and then
is heard a timbre of unusual strength: trail-setter,
shepherd, preacher, comforter,
wisdom teacher such that where he stands
or stood, no less than where he would journey with us,
is holy ground.

ELEMENTAL MUSICS: SELKIRK MOUNTAINS

1. ARIA

Alpine wind
in the stunted firs
half-whispers an austere
wistfulness
with overtones of regret
at being compelled by
a harsh landscape
to be mercilessly forthright:
a breathy flute-note
surging and fading
as the mountain
exhales
   inhales

2. SONATA

The susurrous crescendo
rises amid the crowns of
tall birch, cedar,
pine,
then a diminuendo
erases sound until
the harsh reassurance
swells again where the ridge lifts
from the valley floor:
branches, needles, leaves
paw and tremble at

air, as each trunk-top
gravely pulls the whole edifice
of the tree
into an earthward lean
and back
—the wood nods to
a wind's rhythm

while a grove's worth
of birch and aspen leaves
intricately merges small melodies
until the tunes
cohere as if the rustles
of a human audience
settling into auditorium seats
before a performance
became itself the sonic offering
from the stage: a breezy intricacy
resonant with import,
one hushed theme
a melancholy recognition
of time's disposal of
each of us now living

and another theme, interwoven
under, through, and
around the first's sibilant
strain, invoking
the mysterious, exuberant
and daunting possibilities
that subsume
everything alive.

3. FIRE CREEK

Con anima, con brio

This creek that travels
over stones along a wide channel
between banks of cottonwood,
scrub maple, hemlock
toward the river
releases the vibratos
of a blaze that consists of water
rather than air. The crackling throbs
of the white foam
as the stream cascades
downslope, chord after chord,
in the glittering sun

broadcast in every season
spring's energetic
renaissance: the confidence
of the creek's
sprightly descent, its optimistic
perseverance
at depositing tiny flakes
of gravel,
particle by particle,
in the rocks' lee
until sandy ground
pushes glistening up

into air, to snag a toppled larch,
its still-green branches
trailing in the moving water
—a pianist's hands
that bob over keys—
its trunk thrumming
—a guitarist's
tapping foot.

This waterway's
woodwinds, harmonica
and snare drum
rehearse the stern warbling hiss
of flames'
processional
from source to mouth.

DINO

How can the world go on without Dean Martin
—his crooning voice, maple syrup and butter on slow Sunday
    morning pancakes,
holding back the first word of a lyric phrase not one, not two
but three beats: an easy
whether-you-like-it-or-not assurance
and grace: sly, whimsical, a sonic shrug,
his drawl becoming vibrant only when the words switch to Italian
as if vocalizing *No matter what grades I didn't get in high school,*
buddy, before I dropped out, or where I stand in the pecking order
of the cement crew, I can speak two languages
and am hip to the geography of another country.

                              Dino
Crocetti, born in Steubenville, Ohio,
puddler for the Weirton Steel Company
while launching a welterweight career: *Twelve fights.*
I won all but eleven, he used to joke, juggling a cigarette
and glass on stage—his shtick of being a drunk—
but in truth a family man, preferring to go home after a
    performance
to his wife rather than hit the clubs, the bars.

How can the seasons reappear
with Dean Martin not alive somewhere on the planet
—Palm Beach or Palm Springs or
back in Ohio for all I know.

                    How is the globe able to rotate
and me loading cauliflower into a grocery cart
without my parents to phone or visit, or without pudgy Don
    Hume,

photographer for the student newspaper
when we both worked on it as undergraduates, gone with a heart
  attack,
the first friend of mine who died, or my optometrist,
Eric Beauchamp, whom I saw every year for two decades
and who this May became an obituary
shocking as the space where he was, where they all were,
a gap
the world pretends isn't there, as though they never existed,
as if the earth emerges complete
as it's ever been, each morning I open my eyes.

MINOR

Each minor chord a story
  Tinged with longing yet hopeful:
    Melancholy but

Confident. The sound conveys
  Years past
    —The final shape of what was

Naively wished for—and the years that
  Someone's—my—shortening path
    Still has to wind through.

POP

The songs we moved among,
that I inhabited, suffused me like a marriage

behind me now. If I glance back,
those elated surges—pulses of loss and defiance,

face of the beloved that floated out of
transistors, stylus, dashboard—

appear as a corridor of identical doors
that, if opened, permit a glimpse of lives

that became my life: "Tom Dooley,"
The Kingston Trio; "Wayward Wind," Gogi Grant;

"Come Softly to Me," the Fleetwoods; "I Remember
You," Frank Ifield—each in the moment of its arrival

judged, absorbed
and added to what I was. I listened with friends

to the newest, until in my thirties
the tunes began to be

randomly encountered, my awareness of the latest
dulled, became patchy,

then blinked out. More than a century ago
railways ran through these high mountains

where I live—passes and valleys linking the smelters,
mines, concentrators in the 1890s:

all the surveying of routes, construction of ingenious trestles,
cuts and fills, the blur of monotonous, dangerous labour

with ties and ballast, fishplates and rails
vanished, the right-of-ways sold

or overgrown with aspen and fir
—no one alive remembering the schedules, stations, sheds

long ago collapsed under heavy snow.
But in their time

these railroads were river and highway,
were tobacco and salt,

a Bible verse familiar since childhood,
a warm canyon wind through the afternoon.

THE TABLE

How old the wind sounds
in its weary passes through the pine branches
at the edge of a grove.
In each dying hiss are millions of years
surging through grass,
and driving rain high on the ridgetops
above the valleys, dust
along the lakeshore

—an exhaustion
which vibrates too in the long harmonica solo
with drums and guitar under
that drive the tune forward
while the musician, even with the harp at his lips,
thinks how soon it will be three a.m.
and he will leave the club, stepping onto the sidewalk
wet from rain now ended, street lamps
casting their long reflections of light
in the asphalt's puddles. No one around.
November already, another year.
He'll keep his chilled hands in his old coat
for the half-hour walk to the apartment
unless a late bus comes by
when he's near a stop. Indoors
he will sit at the white kitchen table
for hours, as though behind the wheel
on a windy highway to somewhere, some gig
perhaps, or a visit to his brother, sipping tea
or a whiskey while the music slowly settles,
ebbs from his mind
until the darkness, breath by breath
surrenders the room's appliances and counters
to a pale light
that seeps into the world
another time.

SONG: EAGLE IN THE AIR

Eagles in their feathery
explosion of desire

soar toward each other, lock legs
like galaxies merging,

and drop
hundreds of meters, spinning in a fierce

compaction of selves
that plunges, swirls

toward a ridge of spruce
far below, or cottonwood and aspen

along the river:
the rotating treetops

pulse dizzily toward them
in their voraciousness to

touch, stroke, enter every part of
each other's whirling bodies, until

a second before impact
we burst into

the ecstatic surge that propels
two universes into birth

who separately expand to flap away
over water meadow and summit

circling each other as we achieve
altitude, coasting

into distinct skins, faces, hair
though all night we lie

entwined, moon
a crescent long sunk under

the mountain, so in a star-lit afterdark,
scent of balsams and newly turned earth,

we sleep in the shadow
of the Milky Way.

DIAGNOSIS

A diagnosis appears in a family's news
    —An illness whose pleas for cash before

Were unseen by them: a mortal disease that is spread
    By pathogens crossing the ridges and alpine meadows

Airborne, to germinate where opportunity
    Is fertile

In the upper and lower motor neurons
    Of the spinal cord, or in the meninges

Or adrenal glands, as a trout species
    Manifests in a new meltwater course

On the mountain, these fish identical
    To ones in the closest stream

A forest removed. Or, as on a snow-covered sandbar
    In the river valley, a hawk stumps side to side,

Half-hops as she opens and retracts her left wing,
    Feathers of the other tight against her body.

Standing just beyond the span of a lunge,
    If the hawk were able still to lunge,

An eagle abruptly rises, fluttering, to overtop the hawk.
    Beak, talon slash the prey

Despite her attempts to dodge. The eagle
    Settles out of reach,

Watches the smaller predator
    Absorb the latest agony

—Spreading and releasing feathers that still work,
    Legs adjusting pain into another position—

Until her tormentor launches once more into air, delivering
    A strike the hawk partially avoids,

Partially receives, the attacker alighting on snow
    On the victim's other side, poised

As if to guard the hawk from harm:
    The eagle patient, implacable.

Along the bank,
    A dozen tundra swans and their young

Disregard the assassination, float
    On the current, release their bugled cry or song,

Or stand on the frozen shore
    To feed or find food, to assume

The day we each
    Have been brought to.

HELPLESS ANGELS

A trumpet's fierce groan
unspools across the night roofs
an alloy of copper and gold
extruded to one long cry: a gleaming, undulating wire
while hesitant
                    first raindrops
touch pavement
seconds before the drum's downpour: roiling sheets
of gale water
hammer on windows, siding, shingles
as a reed in a silver mouthpiece
cold presses air: autumnal notes
that amid the storm convert to
flecks of transparent light
through which wander crystalized small cubes
of sound from the keys of
an opalescent piano
—the audible sparks
smelling of rained-on kelp, barnacled
stones, rotted sea wrack amid tufts of
spume grass, calls of gulls and oystercatchers
and the inexorable rhythmic clamour
of the surf: the bass
insisting *mine, mine*
and *every knee shall bow*

                    But the trumpet's
solitary flight
once released
mounts unrecallable above the black streets'
carpet of lamps,
buses, lone sedans, taxis
splashing down avenues that reek of
diesel, malt, sawdust

while the hunched neck of a sodden-coated
walker passes: love's mourner
or late-shift absentee
intent on surcease, balm
with hair and skin soaked
except for hands clenched in wet pockets
as each squelching step between the concrete's
pools and rivulets
conveys him or her toward hope of refuge,
warmth

yet the trumpet's phosphorescent ascent
drags behind it a weariness
that drum, sax, piano, bass
also attest to: these helpless angels
retreating upstream from grief, wrongs, bearing
that sadness aloft
to gaze down on the tower tops of
the immense river bridge, strands and railings
formed from beams of light, austere arcs
that across dark water
lift a shushing of rubber, metal, glass
to a final arpeggio:
feathers of a dripping crow
that on the terminal shore
glides from cedar to cedar,
its wings starting to whisper
applause

THE SONG

I

Now she inhabits only one season
An end to pain

took her from sweaty travel on skis
up a tracked winter trail

the chilled flesh of too long swimming in a lake
one July afternoon

Her season remains without variation
or change

as if she had become a word: a language's
inscribed letters or sounds

II

Where the forest's snow
extends to the river

the flow between white shores
is not much wider than a creek

this January: the water
in places barely covers the stones

that while the current passes
repeat her name—vowels and consonants

that mean
another thing to the river

III

Dense mist in the snowy branches
of cedar and spruce

settles as a fog on Lebahdo's fields
until it abruptly lifts

to reveal fence lines
grove of cottonwood trunks

So her face
suddenly clears out of memory's neuronal haze

with her hand
that reaches to touch someone's arm

while she speaks, and the rhythm
of her body when she crosses a room

IV

Where does the music go
when a song one loves to hear

ends, the humming silence and
discordance of the world

reimposed? The song
The song

THIRTEEN WAYS OF LOOKING AT ROBERT ZIMMERMAN

Bob Dylan

1

How far in, he said
do you want to go?

2

At the edge of adulthood, we believed him alongside us
as we doubted the chanted admonishments
of church, school, the men with guns
keeping us, they declared, free *The words that are used*
he strummed *for to get the ship confused*
will not be understood as they're spoken
And *Your sons and your daughters*
are beyond your command

3

He jeered, though
as we wouldn't
at who hurt him in love *You just kinda wasted*
my precious time Pain
when one we wanted we couldn't have
he transformed to a gloat
as we applauded: the formerly desired
now a loser *How does it feel?*
He hammered those who didn't love us
or love us enough
with the revenge of the future *time*

will tell just who fell
And who's been left behind

4

Forever oppositional
he aligned with no faction, no tendency
beyond evasion or mockery of
behavior, beliefs expected
even of him: an electric folk song
the duet with that redneck pro-war
Johnny Cash

5

If she wakes up now, she'll just want me to talk
I got nothin' to say, 'specially about whatever was

6

He never had an 8:30 history class
away across campus
all winter He never punched in
morning after morning
through spring and summer
But he could sing clockwatching
X-ing the days, the wish for retribution
for the choices we were compelled
to make *I remember every face*
of every man who put me here

7

On his knees
back bent to stare eye to eye
at a chicken

on *Self Portrait*, standing bent forward from the waist
to peer out along the sidewalk
from the bottom of an ascending stairwell on
Street Legal

8

Consistently apocalyptic about floods
like Noah or any other ark survivor
with PTSD *Water pourin' into Vicksburg*
Don't know what I'm going to do
"Don't reach out for me," she said
"Can't you see I'm drownin' too?"
High water everywhere In the dream
he goes down
or under *If it keeps on rainin'*
the levee gonna break
Some of these people gonna strip you of all they can take

9

The Ohio, the Cumberland, the Tennessee
. . . them rebel rivers

10

Jesus shows up on stage
—in that *creation where one's nature*
neither honors nor forgives
another Jewish contrarian
like Lucifer, determined neither to serve
in Hell or Heaven

Lots of sex in fundamentalist churches
according to Bob Garrison Every so often
Garrison would flip out, check himself

into a psych ward for a few weeks When he was released
he'd join a congregation, enjoy
lots of fucking *Oh, sister*
when I come to knock on your door
then quit, be again standing on asphalt
He looked into her eyes when she stopped him to ask
if he wanted to dance; he had a face like a mask

11

Country pie tasted of
the all-night café beside the river
before the freeway starts to lift
into foothills *where the trucks are rollin' slow*

Tired horses graze in the sunny pasture
Moon over barren fields, frost on the window
Behind the wheel of the Silverado, late for afternoon shift
at the mill

12

The empty table on the beach
at which cross-eared surrealists sit
to reload shotguns

or manipulate marionettes to throw stones
at the train of fools
caught in a nearby energy field

L=A=N=G=U=A=G=E
= *call me any name*
you like

"Floater" the perfect American ghazal
And the lyrics altered
in every live performance

13

His notes, his rhythms permeate the journey
—pistons, tires, the wind over the hood
fenders *I'm taking you with me, honey baby*
Sheets of rain falling
that Wednesday lost in Chihuahua, Mexico
after the "Before the Flood" tour, *señor*

Or a mile outside Amarillo
Texas, at Henry Porter's wrecking yard
Ruby describes a rigged swap meet
If she and Henry are married
did Henry on the licence use his real name?
The singer tells her he and his companion
plan to drive *'Til the sun peels the paint
and the seat covers fade
'Til the wheels fall off and burn*
But that's just snake talk

He's going, we're going in
where the music coming from

DESCENDING BLUES

Chord traverses to
chord, as the highway
switchbacks down
from Silverton summit
curve after curve.
The forested mountain-
side—spruce, pine,
hemlock—fills the windshield
—also birch, cottonwood
—with each turn
under a blue
summer sky. The music
accompanying the two-lane's
abrupt
corners is
a beautiful consolation
for and fashioned of
loss and pain; the swaying
rhythm matches
the asphalt's shifts
of motion, always
lower
and lower toward the still-
invisible lake.
The singer's lyrics
between the leaves, cutbank
and drop-off
form a thought
sad and triumphant
in its grief, release
—a route
through the mind, the steep
grade frictionless, winding

until knotted at the sharp
angles or key
changes, then restored
momentarily to a fluid
forward pulse
followed by another
braking, a pause
that drops irredeemably
through time
crying *farewell*
fare well

ENGINEER

for Jesse Winchester

Wintry November night beyond the café windows
in Vernon, while indoors
a rhythm guitar, upright bass
and the long neck of Neil Fraser's lead guitar
point the direction for the stave to go.
Neil's fingers, wood and strings
abruptly release five parallel lines
to race outward, unrolling in synch
across the valley, pastures, mountains
east of town: the five tracks
undulate, twist, sway together
as they traverse cutbanks, fills,
leap ditches and gullies,
pound by orchards of bare trees,
stubbled cornfields,
dodge cliffs too massive to dynamite,
and lift between massed pines and firs
draped with snow in the chill air.
Close behind, Neil's blurred hands
control the great locomotive
whose leading truck of five wheels abreast
grips the bucking, heaving lines
that hurtle through the dark
while the vast machine of sound pulls the room, pulls us all
wheeled and traveling down the route, the engine's
headlamp beam
piercing the blackness.

Isn't that so?

Neil, grimacing, peers forward
as he launches now and then
baseball-size globes of light

to float above him, fading, dreamy.
But more often he propels
flocks and salvos of other radiances
far ahead into the black terrain:
intricate pyrotechnics, fleets
of skyrocketing glowing projectiles,
tracer shells, star shells
that flash-illuminate the path seconds before
the first of the loco's wheels
follow the banking, leveling, tilting again
ribbons of the stave.

                  One cluster
of the quick-fired small globes
arcs ahead beyond the rushing sound to dance
over a gulch or canyon
while the lights wait for more of their kind
to reach them. The assembled group
drops to spin into a circle before forming
above the rift in the earth
a bridge of light: a span at whose supported deck
the hard-driving lines of the stave
arrive in a moment and cross, the locomotive
following seconds later
and the instant the trailing wheels of the passenger car
in which the rest of us ride reach ground on the farther side
the lights wink out, the bridge
evaporates as from Neil's strings
more lights shoot forward to

flare over the stave as it curves
through a snow-laden forest.

Isn't that so?

And what of the expanse of rock, ice,
white field and mountain range
that the notes and chords, the pulses of the wheels
bear us toward? Dark branches of the evergreens,
dark rises of stone that edge the dark ravines
the unspooling stave races past
below indifferent summits
—the sound not knowing where else to take us
but further into winter
while the shifting, bending flow of the lines
soars across or speeds beside water
frozen, or darkly running
like the music, the music.

Isn't that so?

"I MIGHT NOT, MIGHT NOT FEEL THIS GOOD AGAIN"

Phoebe Snow (1950-2011)

A note, purer
        than candlelight

formed from a person's
        skill, not a machine

product:
        white haze

of a fine fall of snow
        against the distant cedar's, fir's

dark green, branch tips
        fringed in white

The sound
        ageless, like light

—young when released, when the chords
        began travelling

and thereafter no older:
        the light, streaking toward me

from a star's cauldron,
        unsullied, unchanged

while its maker,
        infinitely far in time,

sickens, exhausted,
        bloats, hemorrhages,

        collapses
The sung tone,

a wave, a stream of
        moments,

proceeds across that echoing gulf,
        vibrating with

the sad courage
        of being born

LIKE WATER, MUSIC

> *el agua . . .*
> *no se consume como el fuego sangriento*
> *no se convierte en polvo ni en ceniza*
>
> —Pablo Neruda, "Fin de fiesta, VIII"

1

Like water, music neither consumes as a fire does
nor transforms to dust and ash.

Resembling water in one of its states,
a cantata can drift through air
though unlike water, a hymn cannot in any configuration
be channeled across a landscape

despite how both music and water
may be harnessed to generate a desired effect
while retaining a pristine form.

2

Water is older than music's earthly home.
Yet the art is ancient enough:
our bodies are mostly water
like the planet
and melody was taught to each of us in the womb
by a young woman's heart.

Indeed, the human throat and mouth
are shaped as much for music
as for any other utterance. Sung words
were perhaps coincident with speech
—one thinks of those stutterers

who nonetheless can mellifluously
sing.

When winter fog
hovers over white fields here, shelves of ice
materialize at the edges of the rivulets and creeks
that thread out of the mountainside spruce and cedar forest.

So, too, fingers absently strumming guitar strings,
or an ear that absorbs a sequence of heard or
imagined sounds, or a hand scribing time-signature changes
onto a sheet of lined staves
are transubstantiated
by a mind into harmonies, contrapuntal rhythms, ballads

while above the ridges
float enormous clouds
—vast reservoirs of future music.

TWO MOUNTAIN SONGS

1. STONE

Stand tall,
Granitic strata

Levered upright, vertical,
From sea-bed, cragged top

Snow-dusted this month
—Massif so huge and high

That firs and pines
Climbing your slopes to bare rock

Are green stain. Stand:
You were molten once,

Then cooler, pliable, heaved
Into air

Then far, far aloft.
Yet you shall be

Abraded low, shall even
Melt again.

Yet while I live
You are mountain.

Wonder. Vast stone
Defiant of time's ice,

Time's fire—for now.
Stand tall, mountain.

2. SNOW BEES

Molecules of air
Annealed to white flakes
Drift, clump in a swirl
Above black asphalt:

Dense white cloud
Of specks that like waxwings
Rise, deke right, drop, undulate,
Spiral skyward.

Below the immense wall
Of the Rockies' Main Range
Between Kootenay Crossing and Mount Hector,
White bees buzz from a dark sky.

The peaks that line this passage:
White. Roadside meadows: white.
Glacial river on the valley bottom:
White. But a black route curves ahead

Through a white swarm
Of tumultuous air.

TO HOLD FROM THIS DAY FORWARD

In our best clothes, we assemble
to solemnize this union

Several guests in turn address the gathering
The voices of a few speakers

are interrupted by silence for a breath or longer
due to incipient tears

even though such talkers also recount
various humorous antics of the bride or groom

All in attendance are relatives or friends
of only one half of this couple

No one here has any association
with the groom's or the bride's spouse

So whoever speaks today
during the ceremony or reception

tells no anecdotes about the spouse
Nobody really knows the spouse

—only what the spouse does
That the latter is a bigamist

is understood, but never mentioned
since we are aware that at some point

the spouse's name will be linked to ours
As with any wedding, there is an individual

—or more than one—devastated
because his or her hopes

for a future intimacy with the bride or groom
are shattered by this occasion

Such a man or woman, inconsolable at the moment
may or may not be in the hall

Indeed, neither of the nuptial couple is with us
Music performed at the ceremony, however,

whether a contemporary, religious
or classical composition

constitutes selections the organizers of the event
believe the groom or bride would want played

That the spouse is not drawn to music
is recognized by those who compiled the program

Nor has the spouse
or the other matrimonial partner

identified a desired present to honour their union
The family of the bride or groom

may publish details of a gift registry
based on their relative's experiences

yet no information is forthcoming
from the spouse's side

Many guests
simply send flowers

SLIPPERY WIND

1

Tree limbs' ends
reach to grasp the slippery wind: needles of balsam, hemlock,
scaly cedar feathers strive
to seize the air rocking them, flurry of birch leaves
lifted and dropped tries to grab
hold, slow the gale,
tame it
back

2

Fingers of the branches' tips
play the fluid instrument of the wind
note upon note, a music mostly beyond
or below the spectrum
of the human ear: chord sequences so piercing and
sweet they summon clouds
five times the dimensions
of the mountains that edge this valley
The airy structures with their dark interiors
—cumulo, strato, nimbo—
are drawn by the melody to first peer, then rise
over the summits, to pause
transfixed by the tune the forested slopes beneath
release, to let down
drops of moisture the trees need

> A thundering veil descends
> on creek bed, stony outcrop
> —the ridges' storms of shaking aspen,
> swaying pine and spruce
> a music justified

INSTRUMENTAL

A landscape can also be music. South of Eugene
        on the freeway, slopes of second growth lift
to become densely wooded buttes, each with a counterpoint of
    draws, creeks,
        cliffs, deer and, above the spiky horizon, hawks

that circle on the thermals. When the four-lane ascends straight up
    a mountain,
        the terrain's tones and harmonies crescendo
while those of tires, engine, wind over metal
        diminish. But once the asphalt summits

and descends, forest, hillside, meadows subside
        to, at last, the low bass line of the river glinting between
cottonwood and oak on the valley floor, as melodies of wheels,
    pistons
        and airflow sound ever louder. Then a bridge deck drums
         a few bars

before the vehicular ensemble quiets,
        a ridge's chord progression swells, one more time.

ONE MORE TIME

First guitar chords, first words
from the singer

and the paved two-lane
curves once more up into autumn
hills of massed firs and hemlocks
speckled with golden blurs of larch

amid which the road lifts, descends
and climbs again across
the cloudy day, creek beds and
cooling ridges
that together constitute
the land now lost: the shut door
unanswered appeal
rejection letter
a silence
on the phone
the dread diagnosis
packed suitcases and boxes

—the singer's voice soars and falls
transmuting a sweetness from such pain

as from the lover's skin, knolls and
declivities, secret moisture

until the guitar notes reach
snow: a high brown meadow that whitens
in the season's first storm, where the pines
towering beside the fences of this field
hold within themselves, despite buffetings
of icy wind, the gift
they will wait forever to release
at the right time

STORM MUSIC

Those electric guitar notes
that hover in air
each one reverberating with an energy

that pulses with a mysterious
imperative *You better listen*
if you know what's good for you

then lurches forward a bar or two
as another tone arrives
which also pauses to resonate *Be warned*

are the white storm
that obscures a ridgeline
of the valley wall

and that blurs a spur's summit below
while the fir and spruce slopes
of the dark mountain itself

whose upper gullies, avalanche chutes
and rock faces
endure blizzard or driving rain

are an organ's series of chords
somber but implacable
attesting *Gale, heavy snowpack, icy mist*

cannot frighten or dismay a faith
that rears so far aloft
from lake and river valley

that will prevail Yet the peaks are lost
behind the vibrating notes, under a cloud of
sleet, a perilous beauty

WHEELBARROW LULLABY

As a December
afternoon dims, I
roll you under
the woodshed's open
roof again and
turn to go.
Hour after hour
you and I
trundled firewood from
the stack piled
in June heat
round the house
on a path
cut through snow
to the basement's
door and inside
to unload and
stack there. Then
back out to
the cold once
more. The short
winter day is
ending, both of
us are tired
from our long
labours. So I
park you here,
out of the
weather, wish you
a pleasant sleep
until tomorrow. We
have been through
much, old friend:

hauling in spring
earth, manure, trees
for planting, sacks
of mulch, trays
of flower and
veggie starts. In
summer, firewood to
the shed, stones
from the field.
In autumn, bags
of leaves and
the harvest: squash,
carrots, cukes. I
leave you now,
as darkness deepens
in the snowy
forest around, to
whatever wheelbarrows dream
of: being brand-new
with tray unmarked
and handles unworn,
or rolling free
of every burden,
or bearing marvels
into the light.

SUNDAY NIGHT

Death is the mother of beauty; hence from her,
Alone, shall come fulfilment to our dreams
And our desires.

— Wallace Stevens, "Sunday Morning"

I think not: the spruce's tiers of branches
rise like a song—each level's array
of needles, twigs, upturned end
of downward-sloping limbs
smaller than those beneath
so the living plant tapers
toward an impossible height
—an ascending projectile's green exhaust
that cones outward
as the missile surges into a blue sky.

Or maybe? Death does clear off
or make use of
the old. The elements, even of our bodies,
originate in a dead star.
But the provision of a locale and materials
is not mothering. For any species
able to comprehend an aesthetic,
life arises from life: the air jammed
with floating snowflakes,
a rainbow lifting in a steep arc
from a mountainside.

Thus, no. A house-wall-high, wall-wide
curtain of yellow forsythia: should we anoint the bee
its mother? The mind
is the mother of beauty: *momentary,*
the poet said elsewhere, as our species

is momentary in the cosmos' eye,
as the universe itself may exist briefly
in energy's reckoning,
to light's mindless mind. And if all time
can only be what we living comprehend,
death is the end of beauty.

Eyes glimmering softly
in a loved face
over a table, or remembered.

A hummingbird poised
on vibrating air.

THE HEART STOPS, BUT NEVER THE MUSIC

The melody's, harmony's notes,
an undulating line of multicolored beads
illuminated from within,
travel toward me: a series
of giant photons of every hue
with more forming in air where the progression starts.
Each glowing droplet
vanishes the instant it impacts my eardrum
and is absorbed, releasing tiny jolts of pleasure:
endorphins of light.

> When I spend an evening alone to hear
> the tunes, lyrics, vocal shadings I love,
> time spreads out
> distant as my mind can reach
> while the room's walls and ceiling
> turn translucent, then vanish.
> The chord progressions, sung verses
> buoy me out into a landscape
> dense with hope, with grief, with beauty

—a terrain I also enter when
speeding along asphalt
my voice behind the steering wheel fills the cabin
with song: the road I navigate,
past farmsteads, orchards, exits to small towns,
exuberant with music

> —a transitory substance
> that quantifies and arranges
> the minutes' indivisible flow:
> a space in the mind cleared and furrowed
> to yield the sustenance we require.
> From our first hours, we are sung to sleep
> —that primal comfort—and throughout our days,

our decades awake, we continue listening
while the ceaseless beat, tones, cadences,
sing us toward
the unending night.

Music is the laughter of
consciousness
—now pure joy, now
indulgent, now mocking,
regretful, impressed
—always
a communion
with wonder.

A MUSIC

1

A music
sounded through the valley

one evening in late summer
Drums of course

and the journey of a flute
climbing and descending a path

into these mountains
companioned by the vibration

of electrified strings: sequences of
chords and single tones

that wavered between silences
—tree frogs summoning the darkness

2

The music
was lovely

but night here is prowled by wood rat
and not love, by snake, a sudden scudding of deer

amid skunk stink, the dread of
bear: spikes of menace

formed of black air
left when the moon sets

—air in which the invisible road

pushes past cottonwood, aspen, vine maple

3

To restore the ordinary night, I
steered my house across the valley

With only the building's running lights on
I kept the small blaze of sound astern

until at the base of the western ridge
I anchored where firs, pines and cedars

shadowed a dark shoreline
Around my dwelling I set out my lawns

and secured them to fencing, deck stairs and doorway
While ripples of distant melody

nudged at the hull of the vessel
my beds of delphinium, columbine, strawflower

stood watch through the mute bells
that mark the hours

And when the east at last brightened
the waters stilled

Now I could see that the music
had brought me to moor in the hum audible

at the core of quiet
as though in the black fires on the face of the sun

or amid a new weather
Surrounded by all I was used to

I had reached a country
strange to me as my life

THE FUTURE

A square of bright moonlight
on the kitchen tiles.
Outside, as the white disk
burns in the blackness
my lawns could be snow-covered
but aren't.

Early spring again:
tulips and hyacinths
only an inch of green leaf
above the mulch
—the beds a tumult of shadows
under the stars.

I never want a story
to end. You are ash.
I remember
there is no future
but I remember how you enchanted
and exasperated me.

There is no future
for me, either.
Hard moonlight
on white tiles
and the greening
grass. Without a future

the story stops.
The moon just past full.

SHELBY WALL AND JOHN LENT PERFORM 12-BAR BLUES AT THE UPSTAIRS, VERNON, BC

February snowfall outside the big front windows
this evening: the dense array of flakes suspended
as the rhythm of the struck strings of Shelby's guitar, insistence
of the troubled soul John's lyrics inhabit,
propel the streets and roofs steadily upwards
through white tufts, like a car on a night highway
amid a snowstorm that, in the headlamps,
rushes at the windshield
—except, as the driving wheel of the verses
cycles again, the words, the chords
draw the jammed room, each building, the town
higher out of the gravity well.

                              Note by note
we rise through hours
into sparser and sparser air. The sun will fail,
galaxies will fail, the fabric of this universe
will spread and dim, or collapse to an infinite weight
and yet we sang: flint sparked fire,
we hammered steel into steel,
found the recipe for bread, ploughed
the same field for forty years.
Fletcher, cooper, wainwright,
typewriter repairer, it was messy,
it mattered, it didn't matter. We lift into nothing
trailing behind us the lost chants, incantations,
war cries, denunciations, love charms,
languages, harmonies: it was messy,

it mattered, it didn't matter. These are what we made
as we ascended amid the snow, as our dwellings travelled
up toward the greater night.

                        We couldn't do nothing.
Here where memory simplifies,
weakens and is gone, we couldn't stop,
we ascended outward to the dark, it didn't matter, we
sang.

ACKNOWLEDGEMENTS

Much gratitude to the editors and staff of the following journals that published (sometimes in earlier forms) or have accepted poems in this collection.

Arc: "One Time"; "Heavy Weather"
Canadian Literature: "Like Water, Music"
Cloudbank: "Pop"
Contemporary Verse 2: "Slippery Wind"
Dalhousie Review: "I Might Not, Might Not Feel This Good Again"; "A Music"
Denver Quarterly: "One More Time"
Event: "Instrument"; "Song"
Exile: "Engineer"
FreeFall: "Sunday Night"
Hanging Loose: "Dino"; "The Future"
Hayden's Ferry Review: "Blue North"
Hubbub: "Descending Blues"
Hudson Review: "Helpless Angels"; "To Hold from This Day Forward"
I-70 Review: "Instrumental"
Lime Hawk's anthology, *Trailhead: Literature for the Backcountry*: "Song: Eagle in the Air"
Miramar: "Richie Havens"
New Orphic Review: "Thirteen Ways of Looking at Robert Zimmerman"
Prairie Fire: "Fred Neil and the Rainbow"; "Shelby Wall and John Lent Perform 12-Bar Blues at the Upstairs, Vernon, BC"
Queen's Quarterly: "The Table"; "Wheelbarrow Lullaby"
Windfall: "Diagnosis"